MARS
and the
Seventh Trumpet

RANDY SHIRLEY

ISBN 978-1-64140-839-4 (paperback)
ISBN 978-1-64140-840-0 (digital)

Christian Faith Publishing, Inc.
832 Park Avenue
Meadville, PA 16335
www.christianfaithpublishing.com

Printed in the United States of America

Chapter 1

Solomon said in Ecclesiastes 7:8, "The end of a thing is better than its beginning" (NKJV). That is the reason I am going to give you the conclusion of all that I am about to say first. Revelations 21:3–7 says, "And I heard a loud voice from heaven saying, 'behold, the tabernacle of God is with men, and He will dwell with them, and they shall be His people. God Himself will be with them and be their God. And God will wipe away every tear from their eyes; there shall be no more death, nor sorrow, nor crying. There shall be no more pain, for the former things have passed away.' Then He who sat on the throne said, 'Behold, I make all things new.' And He said to me, 'Write, for these words are true and faithful.' And He said to me, 'It is done! I am the Alpha and the Omega, the Beginning and the End. I will give of the fountain of the water of life freely to him who thirsts. He who overcomes shall inherit all things, and I will be his God and he shall be my son'" (NKJV). These are promises made by our Creator. Think about these verses as you read this book, and remember, it all ends well for believers.

Late one afternoon in August of 2003, I went outside to walk around in the quiet of the night. I was not searching for anything, just a nice walk and a view of the night sky. Living in the country affords you the privilege of seeing the stars without all the glare of city street lights interfering with the view. On this particular night, I noticed a bright star in the southeastern sky. Most people today are not star gazers as was the case with me, but this was an unusually bright star like a small moon. Many of you reading this may ask what significance could there could be in a bright object in the sky. After all, don't the planets and stars seem brighter and closer at different times? Well, not this bright and not this large.

I went out for the next several nights and continued to see this same bright star in the sky like a small moon. Like many other people, I put it in the back of my mind and didn't think much of it for a few years. Then the thought of that star came back to me and would not go away. So I decided to take another look into this strange event and find out what I could about this bright object. After a little research, this object in the sky turned out to be the planet Mars. I've never dwelt on signs in the sky or on the Earth. I have always thought that was for astrologers or some prophet of old to discern, but I had seen it myself, and I was beginning to feel there was some meaning to its appearance. I have read the Bible several times, and I understand that God uses His creation to speak to us if we are looking and listening. Sometimes, even when we are not.

If you are aware, another bright star in the sky appeared about two thousand years ago. Several wise men came to understand that it signified the birth of a king. His name was Yeshua (Jesus), who was born in the land of Israel. I do not know or pretend to know whether the Bethlehem star was a planet such as Venus or a literal star that they saw. What we know for sure is that it was a bright object in the sky. According to modern scientist, the planet Mars hasn't been this close to Earth for many thousands of years, so we can safely rule out that possibility and assume that this significant appearance is a first for Mars in recorded history. Does this appearance mean anything? Is it a sign in the heavens that Jesus spoke about regarding the end time?

After doing some further research on these questions, I believe that this appearance is a sign in the heavens and it does have significant meaning for us today. It also has importance in the near future for the Middle East and here in America as well.

Mars has been the fascination of a great many minds over the last few decades. A lot of speculation has been made about whether or not life has ever been present on its surface or whether aliens have ever landed or lived there. As far back as the ancient Babylonians, the planet has been worshipped as a god (the god of blood). This planet is named after the Roman god of war, Mars, who was worshipped by Augustus Caesar. Augustus was the ruler of the civilized world at the birth of Jesus. So, logically speaking, Mars was the (god of this world) at the time of Jesus birth. Both the old and new testaments of the Bible speak of one to come that would deceive the whole world into believing that he is God. Could this be his star? Is the time of his coming upon us? Is it possible that the appearance of Mars marks the birth of the Antichrist or son of perdition, who is referred to in Daniel Chapter 11 as a man of war? Daniel 11:36–39 says, "Then the king shall do according to his own will: he shall exalt and magnify himself above every god, shall speak blasphemies against the god of gods, and shall prosper till the wrath has been accomplished; for what has been determined shall be done. He shall regard neither the God of his fathers' nor the desire of women, nor regard any god; for he shall exalt himself above them all. But in their place he shall honor a god of fortresses; and a god which his fathers did not know he shall honor with gold and silver, with precious stones and pleasant things. Thus he shall act against the strongest fortresses with a foreign god, which he shall acknowledge, and advance its glory; and he shall cause them to rule over many, and divide the land for gain" (NKJV).

Being a bloody ruler and a man of war is a good description of the mars worshipped by the Babylonians and Mars the god of war, worshipped by Augustus Caesar. He is coming to conquer, rule, and be exalted. Many will be deceived by him into believing he is a god. I believe God will give them over to this delusion because they chose to not believe in Him. In 2 Thessalonians 3:8–12 says, "And then the lawless one will be revealed, whom the Lord will consume with the breath of His mouth and destroy with the brightness of His coming. The coming of the lawless one is according to the working of Satan, with all power, signs, and lying wonders, and with all unrighteous deception among those who perish, because they did not receive the love of the truth, that they might be saved. And for this reason God will send them strong delusion, that they should believe the lie, that they all may be condemned who did not believe the truth but had pleasure in unrighteousness" (NKJV).

Not everyone has taken the time to read the entire books of the Bible and study the prophecies mentioned in them. They get most of what they know about prophesies from movies they watch or a preacher's sermon. I know that I had formed an opinion of how the end times would play out based upon these two things. Jesus would come and rapture us out off Earth before any of the tribulation began. My opinion changed after I read and studied the end times for myself with an open mind.

However, I do agree with most teachers about what the world will look like in the end times. According to the Bible, the conditions of the world indicate we are approaching these times very quickly. Daniel prophesied in Chapter 12, verse 4, that in the last days, knowledge would be greatly increased. That to me seems indisputable. Anyone with knowledge of life on planet Earth one hundred years ago realizes that we are there now. My grandmother told me stories of her and her family traveling to Texas walking beside their horse drawn wagon drinking water from the water barrel. Life was little different for them than what it was two thousand years ago. The world has drastically changed since then. We are definitely living in the information age with the coming of telephones, radios, televisions, and computers.

Anyone with access to a computer has a vast amount of information available to them in just seconds. I can remember researching information at the library in the seventies. It took days to find and read enough information to write a report. Getting that information just a couple of generations ago would have been even more difficult. Today, doing research and solving complex math problems have been made simple with the touch of a few keys on the computer.

Modes of transportation have certainly transformed us into world travelers. Daniel 12:4 also says that in the last days, many will go to and fro in the Earth, which was referring to world travel. I am not sure Daniel realized just how fast that travel would be in a jet plane, helicopter, or cruise ship, but world travel is a common daily occurrence. This prophecy has been fulfilled in the times we now find ourselves. Are there other indicators that would lead us to believe that this is indeed the time of the deceivers coming?

The Apostle Peter predicted: "knowing this first: that scoffers will come in the last days, walking according to their own lust, and saying, 'Where is the promise of His coming? For since the fathers fell asleep, all things continue as they were from the beginning of creation.' For this they willingly forget: that by the word of God the heavens were of old, and the Earth standing out of water and in the water, by which the world that then existed perished, being flooded with water. But the heavens and the Earth which are now preserved by the same word are reserved for fire until the day of judgment and perdition of ungodly men" (2 Peter 3:3–8, NKJV). The scoffers not only doubt prophesies of the Antichrist and the return of the Creator, but they deny the very creation itself with a religion of evolutionary doctrine.

Although there are hundreds of scientist today who believe in a global flood and that the Earth is only a few thousand years old, there are many more who have accepted this last day deception that the Earth was formed billions of years ago through an accidental explosion and there was no global flood four thousand five hundred years ago. They refuse to believe the truth even though fossil graveyards testify of just such a flood.

The Apostle Paul predicted in 2 Timothy 3: "But know this, that in the last days perilous times will come: men will be lovers of themselves, lovers of money, boasters, proud, blasphemers, disobedient to parents, unthankful, unholy, unloving, unforgiving, slanderers, without self control, brutal, despisers of good, traitors, headstrong, haughty, lovers of pleasure rather than lovers of God" (NKJV). That is a perfect picture of our world today. Small town America has even succumbed to this prophesy. I can remember in my lifetime when we never took the keys out of our cars, no matter where we parked for fear of losing them. Today, we take them out when we park in our own garage or when we just run into a convenient store to get a candy bar for fear of someone stealing it. I cannot remember ever locking the front door to our house when we left to go somewhere. It was a secure feeling all the time. Children could safely walk all over town without fear of being abducted. Now we worry about them walking to the mailbox to get the mail. We could leave our children in the living room with the television on any channel without fear of being visually molested by pornographic images or exposed to crude, indecent language. Those days have passed, and a great falling away from morals has occurred in my lifetime. The greatest of our moral declines has been not only the disobedience of children to parents, but the lack of love of parents to the children through neglect, abuse, and the willingness to sacrifice an unborn child for the sake of convenience.

There is a parallel to what is happening in our day and what happened when God sent His two greatest rulers in the past. When the Israelites were in the land of Egypt, a decree was put forth by Pharaoh to cast all the newborn male children whom the parents loved into the river. This is found in Exodus 1:22. This decree to slaughter the children marked the coming of a "great deliverer" who would set the Israelites free. The children were only killed locally, and Moses was a local leader of a specific people. Another forced killing of children occurred with the birth of another "Deliverer" named Jesus. The killing was local and so was the ministry of Jesus. Matthew 15:24 states: "I was not sent except to the lost sheep of the house of Israel" (NKJV). Only after His death was the Gospel message sent into all the world. So, once again, we have the killing of children, except on a global scale, through abortion, and these children are willingly offered up as a sacrifice to financial and emotional gain "selfishness": the god of this world. If this star signifies a coming king, then I submit that he will rule on a global scale and he is here now as a child. He will not be a great "deliverer" but a great "deceiver."

When I first saw this planet in the sky, I wasn't looking for a sign, but a thought did cross my mind. It was something Jesus said in Luke 21:25–27, "And there will be signs in the sun, in the moon, and in the stars; and on the Earth distress of nations, with perplexity, the seas and the waves roaring; men's hearts failing them from fear and the expectation of those things which are coming on the Earth, for the powers of the heavens will be shaken. Then they will see the Son of Man coming in a cloud with great power and glory" (NKJV). I submit that in August of 2003, Mars was a sign in the stars that marked the birth of a conqueror, the Antichrist, and that the nations are perplexed with an onslaught of world terrorism through radical Islamic jihad. Mass immigration throughout the Middle East and even here in America has disrupted the lives of millions of people throughout the world, and many are asking what must be done about it. On top of that, the seas are roaring with tsunamis and hurricanes. We also have volcanoes, earthquakes, famines, and diseases with more destructive force than we have ever seen, and the worst is yet to come. Some people call it climate change. I call it prophecy.

The rise of radical Islam is the most alarming of all these. Predictions I have studied indicate that by the year 2035, the population of Europe along with Great Britain will be over fifty percent Muslim. That would be fine if Islam was indeed a religion of peace, but you need only look at the history of the Middle East to see that there will never be peace there or wherever Islamic fundamentalism is established. Their goal is a world dominated by their religion. The predictions of an Islamic takeover would be in line with the Antichrist coming of age. It's just too obvious to overlook. Part of the end time deception that is being poured out is this ruse that Islam is a religion of peace. Ask any person from the Middle East: What is the punishment for Muslims that accept Jesus as their Savior? The answer is either death or banishment from their families. Ask yourself this question: How long would a pastor in Iran, Iraq, or in Saudi Arabia live if he started a church in one of those countries? Make no mistake. Where Islam rules, either submit to its laws or die. Simple as that.

Jesus did not leave us without any hope, though. If you continue to read verse 28 of Luke 21, He says when we see all these things coming to pass, we are to lift up our heads because our redemption draws near and His return is near. In other words, this coming tragedy will become a beautiful arrangement. He will come to rule and reign in truth and justice for all who look for His return.

Chapter 2

Whether or not you believe the significant appearance of Mars is a sign marking the birth of the Antichrist, all the other prophesies and signs of the end times are very clear. I believe we are at the end of the age that Jesus and the prophets foretold. What will the end of these things look like, and what does the Bible say about the return of Jesus?

Many teach that Christ will return before the rise in power of the Antichrist and all believers will be "raptured" out before the seven-year tribulation period begins. I know that I was taught this (pre-trib) doctrine all of my life and even saw several movies based on this doctrine. Some teach that Christ will return in the middle of the tribulation period (mid-trib). Others proclaim His return at the very end of the tribulation period when the wrath of God is poured out upon the world (post-trib). This is probably the least popular of the three because it involves us having to witness and live or die in the tribulation period. Last of all, there are the unbelievers who deny the things that are happening before their very eyes. If you lived in several places in Africa or the Middle East, you would think you were witnessing the tribulation right now. Christians are being killed for their beliefs and have been for several years. Try preaching in Sudan or Lybia that the tribulation will not begin until Jesus raptures us all away, and they will look at you like you are crazy. The beheadings and the persecutions are going on right now. Just because we are not seeing it here yet, does not mean it is not coming here. We in America have been fortunate and blessed by God with the freedoms we enjoy. If the prophecies made in the Bible are true, then we will soon see tribulation come upon all of the world, including here in America.

I know that this is not what people want to hear. They want to believe that God will not allow us to suffer for His name. I do not believe the church of the last days will escape persecutions, just as the early church did not escape it and many believers throughout history. The apostles of Jesus were imprisoned, beaten, and killed for their faith. The believers in the early churches were persecuted constantly. Paul says in 1 Thessalonians 1:6, "And you became followers of us and of the Lord, having received the word in much affliction." In Revelation 2:8–11, John says, "And to the angel of the church in Smyrna write, these things says the First and the Last, who was dead, and came to life: I know your works, tribulation, and poverty (but you are rich); and I know the blasphemy of those who say they are Jews and are not, but are a synagogue of Satan. Do not fear any of those things which you are about to suffer. Indeed, the devil is about to throw some of you into prison, that you may be tested, and you will have tribulation ten days. Be faithful until death, and I will give you the crown of life. He who has an ear, let him hear what the Spirit says to the churches. He who overcomes shall not be hurt by the second death" (NKJV). I do believe there will be places of refuge and God's protection over many believers. Jesus gives us some words of encouragement in Revelations 3:8–10 saying, "I know your works. See, I have set before you an open door, and no one can shut it; for you have a little strength, have kept My word, and have not denied My name. Indeed I will make those of the synagogue of Satan, who say they are Jews and are not, but lie-indeed I will make them come and worship before your feet, and to know that I have loved you. Because you have kept My command to persevere, I also will keep you from the hour of trial which shall come upon the whole world, to test those who dwell on the earth" (NKJV). There are some believers that will die in the tribulation period. There are others who will not. He's coming back for somebody, so we will not all be killed, but the end times will be rough.

Let me say before I continue that I am not a seminary graduate, nor am I a student of any end time teacher. I am a common laborer and a simple man who knows how to read. I will simply show you what the Bible says and leave the interpretation to you. You may not understand all the symbolism in John's visions, but I think God made the Bible simple enough for all to understand if they simply read what it says. He that has ears to hear, let him hear.

Let's start in 1 Corinthians 15:51 where Paul says, "Behold I tell you a 'Mystery': We shall all be changed, in a moment, in the twinkling of and eye, at the 'last trumpet'. For the trumpet will sound, and the dead will be raised incorruptible, and we shall be changed" (NKJV). Paul does not tell us how many trumpets will blow or what will be happening when it does blow. He simply tells us we shall be changed when the "last" trumpet blows. The verse in 1 John 3:2 tells us, "Beloved, now we are the children of God; and it has not yet been revealed what we shall be, but we know that when He is revealed, we shall be like Him, for we shall see Him as He is" (NKJV). John says we will be changed when we see Jesus, and Paul says that this will happen at the sound of the last trumpet. Now the question is: When will the trumpet blow for us to be "raptured" out?

In Revelation 8:2, John says, "And I saw the seven angels who stand before God, and to them were given seven trumpets." Now we know the number of trumpets and that the last one is the seventh. That could not seem any simpler to me. If you read Revelations Chapter 8 through Chapter 10, you will clearly see that at the sounding of each proceeding trumpet, the wrath of God is poured out in various ways. All these terrible things are happening before the last, or the seventh trumpet blows. I don't see a "rapture" here. Revelation 10:7 says, "But in the days of the sounding of the seventh angel, when he is about to sound, the 'mystery' of God would be finished, as He declared to His servants the prophets" (NKJV). John confirms as Paul does that at the sounding of the seventh (or last) trumpet, the "mystery" of God will be revealed. We will either be raised from the dead or those who remain will be changed into their new bodies. It is no longer a "mystery."

Paul also confirms this once again in 1 Thessalonians 4:15–17: "For this we say to you by the word of the Lord, that we who are alive and remain until the coming of the Lord will by no means precede those who are asleep (dead). For the Lord Himself will descend from heaven with a shout, with a voice of an archangel, and with the 'trumpet' of God. And the dead in Christ will rise first. Then we who are alive and remain shall be caught up together with them in the clouds to meet the Lord in the air. And thus we shall always be with the Lord" (NKJV). Once again, Paul tells us that when the trumpet blows, the dead in Christ will rise and we will be gathered to Him. We have all heard these words read at many funerals, but do we really know that this prophecy is fulfilled at the sounding of the last trumpet? Unless there is another list of trumpets we cannot access, the time line for our rapture is very clear. It is at the end of this age when all things have been accomplished.

Revelation 11:15 says, "Then the seventh angel sounded (talking about the trumpet): and there were loud voices in heaven, saying, 'the kingdoms of this world have become the kingdoms of our Lord and of His Christ, and He shall reign forever and ever'" (NKJV). Jesus takes Lordship over this Earth when the seventh trumpet blows and we are gathered to Him. It all happens at the same time. When the last trumpet blows, that is when we shall be changed and gathered together with Him in the clouds. Paul and John are in agreement with their predictions. I don't see us gathering together at any other trumpet until the last one.

Daniel is in line with what John and Paul are saying. In Daniel Chapter 11, Daniel speaks of the Antichrist rising to power and magnifying himself above all that is called God. Then after the Antichrist, in Chapter 12, he says, "At that time Michael shall stand up, the great prince who stands watch over the sons of your people; and there shall be a time of trouble, such as never was since there was a nation, even to that time. And at that time your people shall be delivered, everyone who is found written in the book. And many of those who sleep in the dust of the earth shall awake, some to everlasting life, some to shame and everlasting contempt. Those who are wise will shine like the brightness of the firmament, and those who turn many to righteousness like the stars forever and ever."

The prophecy in the book Daniel is saying the same thing Paul and John have said: The rise of the Antichrist, then great tribulation, then deliverance, and the raising of the dead in Christ. Don't fall for the last day deception that has been taught by those who darken council by words without knowledge. The mystery will be fulfilled by the believers becoming like Christ in our new bodies. I have yet to find a pre-trib "rapture" in my reading of the Bible.

Paul said in 2 Thessalonians 2:1–5, "Now brethren, concerning the coming of our Lord Jesus Christ and our gathering together to Him, we ask you not to be soon shaken in mind or troubled either by spirit or by word or by letter, as if from us, as though the day of Christ had come. Let no one deceive you by any means; for that Day will not come unless the falling away comes first, and the man of sin is revealed, the son of perdition, who opposes and exalts himself above all that is called God or that is worshipped, so that he sits as God in the temple of God showing himself that he is God. Do you not remember that when I was still with you I told you these things" (NKJV). He says that the coming of the Lord and our gathering together with Him will be after the falling away and the son of perdition (Antichrist) is revealed, not before. Why would the Apostle Paul warn us that the coming of the Lord and our gathering together to Him would come after the Antichrist rises to power if it were not so? So you would not get discouraged when you see the world falling apart and the persecution happening on a global scale. So you would know that our hope is not in this world, but in the One to come. Warnings are not for those who have no chance of seeing it, but for those who will experience it. These words of hope, encouragement, and warning are for this present generation. Things today can change rapidly as we have witnessed many times.

Another end time parable of Jesus comes from Matthew 13:24–30. "The kingdom of heaven is like a man who sowed good seed in his field; but while men slept, his enemy came and sowed tares among the wheat and went his way. But when the grain had sprouted and produced a crop then the tares also appeared. So the servants of the owner came and said to him, 'Sir, did you not sow good seed in your field? How then does it have tares?' He said to them, 'An enemy has done this.' The servants said to him, 'Do you want us then to go and gather them up?' But he said, 'No, lest while you gather up the tares you also uproot the wheat with them. Let both grow together until the harvest, and at the time of harvest I will say to the reapers, 'First gather together the tares and bind them in bundles to burn them, but gather the wheat into my barn'" (NKJV). There will not be two separate harvests. If you take what Jesus said literally, the "rapture" takes place at the same time as the gathering of the wicked. There is no one left to go through another tribulation. It's over. The end.

When Jesus explains the parable to His disciples in Matthew 13:39–43, He says, "The enemy who sowed them is the devil, the harvest is the end of the age, and the reapers are the angels. Therefore as the tares are gathered and burned in the fire, so it will be at the end of the age. The Son of Man will send out His angels, and they will gather out of His kingdom all things that offend, and those who practice lawlessness, and will cast them into the furnace of fire, there will be wailing and gnashing of teeth. Then the righteous will shine forth as the sun in the kingdom of their Father. He who has ears to hear, let him hear" (NKJV). There is only one harvest if you can discern it through the preconceived notions that we have been led to believe. Some of you will absolutely refuse to believe what you are reading because like me, once you have been taught something all your life, it's hard to change your way of thinking. Jesus made it even clearer in Matthew 13:47–50. "Again, the kingdom of heaven is like a dragnet that was cast into the sea and gathered some of every kind, which, when it was full, they drew to shore; and they sat down and gathered the good into vessels, but threw the bad away. So it will be at the end of the age. The angels will come forth, separate the wicked from among the just, and cast them into the furnace of fire. There will be wailing and gnashing of teeth" (NKJV). Jesus made it clear that when He returns, then comes the harvest. This will include the righteous gathering to Him and the unrighteous coming to judgment. I do not see two comings, only one. So where does that leave us in the end times?

Now, most people who believe in a rapture before the coming of the Antichrist cannot imagine a God that would allow His people to remain on Earth during all the plagues and mass killings predicted in the book of Revelations. As I mentioned before, look at the Middle East, North Africa, and now parts of Europe. Many Christians and Muslims are being slaughtered as I write this book. This is the work of a people who feel they are doing the will of God. In John 16:2, Jesus said "They will put you out of the synagogues; yes, the time is coming that whoever kills you will think that he offers God service" (NKJV). Just as the religious leaders of His day did to the disciples, so the fundamental jihadist are doing today. They feel they are doing God a service. Jesus did protect a lot of His followers in the early church, but a good many died. He did not pull them out of harm's way. He encouraged them to have hope. Not in this world, but in the one to come. I know some of this is repetitious, but I cannot state enough the preparations you must make in your hearts and minds to be able to bear what you will witness in these last days. It's always better to be armed with the truth than with religious dogma.

As for the plagues predicted in these last days, remember that the children of Abraham were not taken out of Egypt before the plagues came. They saw the plagues and heard the cries of those who were harmed by them, but God did not allow the plagues to touch any of His people. Just as it was then, so I believe it will be in the tribulation. Psalm 91:1–8 says, "He who dwells in the secret place of the Most High shall abide under the shadow of the Almighty. I will say of the LORD, 'He is my refuge and my fortress: My God in Him will I trust.' Surely He shall deliver you from the snare of the fowler and from the perilous pestilence. He shall cover you with His feathers, and under his wings you shall take refuge; His truth shall be your shield and buckler. You shall not be afraid of the terror by night, nor of the arrow that flies by day, nor of the pestilence that walks in the darkness, nor of the destruction that lays waste at noonday. A thousand may fall at your side, and ten thousand at your right hand; but it shall not come near you. Only with your eyes shall you look, and see the reward of the wicked" (NKJV). I believe this was written for us as an encouragement for what is coming in these last days. God will only pour out His wrath on those who refuse to look to Him for mercy through His Son, Jesus, not on believers.

A lot of (pre-tribbers) base their beliefs on Matthew 24:40–43. "Then two men will be in the field: one will be taken and the other left. Two women will be grinding at the mill: one will be taken and the other left. Watch therefore, for you do not know what hour your Lord is coming. But know this, if the master of the house had known what hour the thief would come, he would have watched and not allowed his house to be broken into"(NKJV).

If this is all I read, this would make sense to believe in a pre-trib rapture, but when you back up to verses 29–31, before this happens, Jesus said, "Immediately after the (tribulation) of those days the sun will be darkened, and the moon will not give its light; the stars will fall from heaven, and the powers of heaven will be shaken. Then the sign of the Son of Man will appear in heaven, and then all the tribes of the earth will mourn, and they shall see the Son of Man coming on the clouds of heaven with power and great glory. And He will send His angels with a great sound of a "trumpet", and they will gather together His elect from the four winds, from one end of heaven to the other" (NKJV). Wow, He talks about gathering us together after the tribulation and the stars falling from heaven. The sun and moon will be darkened, the trumpet will blow, and everyone will see and hear it happen. Looks like the end to me. As you read into Chapter 25, He describes judging the good and the bad after His return. I do not see a rapture here at all until the very end and all has been fulfilled.

After the seventh trumpet has blown in Revelations 11:15, verse 19 says, "Then the temple of God was opened in heaven, and the ark of His covenant was seen in His temple. And there were lightnings, noises, thundering, an earthquake, and great hail" (NKJV). This tumultuous situation is in line with what we just read in Matthew 24. All these things happen at the very end of this age when Christ returns to gather us to Himself.

Not all believers in Christ will agree on how the end times will unfold, but we all agree that Jesus will return as He promised He would. No one knows the day or the hour. The most important thing of all to understand is what Jesus did for us. That He paid the price for our sins on the cross and, upon His return, we will be transformed into His likeness. This is the mystery that has been revealed to us in these last days. That is the hope we have when we witness the lawlessness, deceptions, and the tragedies that are coming upon this world.

I believe all the prophesies made concerning the end times are coming to a conclusion. I believe within the next twenty to thirty years, the Antichrist will be revealed. Are you ready? How do you prepare? Should we stock up on guns and ammo? Might not be a bad idea. Should we stockpile long-lasting food reserves and move to a remote location? That might get you to the seventh trumpet, but what then? How do you prepare for the return of the Creator. How do you prepare for the return of Jesus and the coming day of judgment? Jesus said in Luke 12:4–5, "And I say to you My friends, do not be afraid of those who kill the body, and after that have no more that they can do. But I will show you whom you should fear: fear Him who, after He has killed, has power to cast into hell; yes, I say to you, fear Him!" (NKJV). Jesus is simply letting everyone know there is a judgment day coming for all who dwell on the Earth. Everyone is going to leave this world at some point. They will go when they die or they will go when Jesus returns. The time of preparation is now.

I want you to read a story about a wicked and rebellious king and a prophet of God from I Kings 13:1–30, "And behold a man of God went from Judah to Bethel by the word of the Lord, and Jeroboam stood by the altar to burn incense. Then he cried out against the altar by the word of the Lord, and said, 'O altar, altar! Thus says the LORD: Behold, a child, Josiah by name, shall be born to the house of David; and on you he shall sacrifice the priests of the high places who burn incense on you, and men's bones shall be burned on you.'

And he gave a sign the same day, saying, 'this is the sign which the LORD has spoken: Surely the altar shall split apart, and the ashes on it shall be poured out.' So it came to pass when King Jeroboam heard of the saying of the man of God, who cried out against the altar in Bethel, that he stretched out his hand from the altar, saying, 'Arrest him!' Then his hand, which he stretched out toward him, withered, so that he could not pull it back to himself. The altar also was split apart, and the ashes poured out from the altar, according to the sign which the man of God had given by the word of the LORD. Then the king answered and said to the man of God, 'Please entreat the favor of the LORD your God, and pray for me, that my hand may be restored to me.' So the man of God entreated the LORD, and the king's hand was restored to him, and became as before. Then the king said to the man of God, 'Come home with me and refresh yourself, and I will give you a reward.' But the man of God said to the king, 'If you were to give me half your house, I would not go in with you: nor would I eat bread nor drink water in this place. For so it was commanded me by the word of the LORD, saying, You shall not eat bread, nor drink water, nor return by the same way you came.' So he went another way and did not return by the way he came to Bethel. Now an old prophet dwelt in Bethel, and his sons came and told him all the works that the man of God had done that day in Bethel; they also told their father the words which he had spoken to the king. And their father said to them, 'Which way did he go?' For his sons had seen which way the man of God went who came from Judah. Then he said to his sons, 'Saddle the donkey for me.' So they saddled the donkey for him; and he rode on it, and went after the man of God, and found him sitting under an oak. Then he said to him, 'Are you the man of God who came from Judah?' And he said, 'I am.' Then he said to him, 'Come home with me and eat bread.' And he said, 'I cannot return with you nor go in with you; neither can I eat bread nor drink water with you in this place. For I have been told by the word of the LORD, You shall not eat bread nor drink water there, nor return by the way you came.' He said to him, 'I too am a prophet as you are, and an angel spoke to me by the word of the LORD, saying, Bring him back with you to your house, that he may eat bread and drink water.' (He was lying to him.) So he went back with him, and ate bread in his house, and drank water. Now it happened, as they sat at the table, that the word of the LORD came to the prophet who had brought him back; and he cried out to the man of God who came from Judah, saying, 'This says the LORD: Because you have disobeyed the word of the LORD, and have not kept the commandment which the LORD your God commanded you, but you came back, ate bread, and drank water in the place of which the LORD said to you, Eat no bread and drink no water, your corpse shall not come to the tomb of your fathers.' So it was, after he had eaten bread and after he had drunk, that he saddled the donkey for him, the prophet whom he had brought back. When he was gone, a lion met him on the road and killed him. And his corpse was thrown on the road, and the donkey stood by it. The lion also stood by the corpse. And there, men passed by and saw the corpse thrown on the road, and the lion standing by the corpse. Then they went and told it in the city where the old prophet dwelt. Now when the prophet who had brought him back from the way heard it, he said, 'It is the man of God who was disobedient to the word of the LORD. Therefore the LORD had delivered him to the lion, which has torn him and killed him, according to the word of the LORD which He spoke to him.' And he spoke to his sons, saying, 'Saddle the donkey for me.' So they saddled it. Then he went and found his corpse thrown on the road, and the donkey and the lion standing by the corpse. The lion had not eaten the corpse not torn the donkey. And the prophet took up the corpse of the man of God, laid it on the donkey, and brought it back. So the old prophet came to the city to mourn, and to bury him. Then he laid the corpse in his own tomb; and they mourned over him, saying, 'Alas, my brother!'" (NKJV).

The first twenty times I read this story, I was upset with God about the whole shady deal. Why did God so harshly judge the godly prophet while giving the wicked king mercy? Then about thirty years after first reading this, it came to me that the wicked king had asked for mercy, but I cannot find where the prophet ever entreated the Lord's favor or mercy. He did not ask for it. Simple as that. Jesus said in Matthew 7:7–8, "Ask and it will be given you; seek, and you will find; knock, and it will be opened to you. For everyone who asks receives, and he who seeks finds, and to him who knocks it will be opened" (NKJV). God is not a respecter of persons. The prophet did not ask, and he did not receive. Many people today never ask God for mercy or forgiveness of their sins. They just think that if they are good enough, they will go to heaven. They are wrong. The Apostle Paul says in Romans 3:23, "for all have sinned and fallen short of the glory of God" (NKJV). Isaiah 64:6 says, "But we are all like an unclean thing, And all our righteousnesses are like filthy rags" (NKJV). In other words, we are as dirt before God, and all the good things we could possibly do in this world will not make us pure before Him. Making ourselves pure is beyond our power. We have to ask for it. That request is made possible through what Jesus did on the cross around two thousand years ago. He died on that cross to make us pure.

I want to tell you another story about an event that happened to the Israelites when Moses was leading them through the desert after their freedom from Egypt as slaves. Numbers 21:4–9 says, "Then they journeyed from Mount Hor by Way of the Red Sea, to go around the land of Edom; and the soul of the people became very discouraged on the way. And the people spoke against God and against Moses: 'why have you brought us up out of Egypt to die in the wilderness? For there is no food and no water, and our soul loathes this worthless bread.' So the LORD sent fiery serpents among the people, and they bit the people; and many of the people of Israel died. Therefore the people came to Moses, and said, '"We have sinned, for we have spoken against the LORD and against you; pray to the LORD that He take away the serpents from us.' So Moses prayed for the people. Then the LORD said to Moses, 'Make a fiery serpent, and set it on a pole; and it shall be that everyone who is bitten, when he looks at it shall live.' So Moses made a bronze serpent, and put it on a pole; and so it was, if a serpent had bitten anyone, when he looked at the bronze serpent, he lived" (NKJV).

That was an illustration of a people doomed to death. They were incapable of saving themselves from the judgment of God, but they asked for mercy and mercy was given. They obtained life and forgiveness by believing God and looking to Him for deliverance. I wonder sometimes how many people perished that thought looking at a snake on a pole was a dumb idea. They probably stayed at home doing good works to make themselves presentable to God. They died. Only God's way is acceptable to Him. Jesus said in the book of John 3:14–21, "And as Moses lifted up the serpent in the wilderness even so must the Son of Man be lifted up, that whoever believes in Him should not perish but have eternal life. For God so loved the world that He gave His only begotten Son, that whoever believes in Him should not perish but have everlasting life. For God did not send His Son into the world to condemn the world, but that the world through Him might be saved. He who believes in Him is not condemned; but he who does not believe is condemned already, because he has not believed in the name of the only begotten Son of God. And this is the condemnation, that the light has come into the world, and men loved darkness rather than light, because their deeds were evil. For everyone practicing evil hates the light and does not come to the light, lest his deeds should be exposed. But he who does the truth comes to the light, that his deeds may be clearly seen, that they have been done in God."

So God made another pole called a cross. He put up another object on a pole. That object was His Son who paid the price for all our sins with His death upon that cross. You need only look to His Son on that cross to be healed. Why would anyone throw away such an opportunity to escape the judgment of God coming upon all the world. You can keep trying to be good enough to get into heaven by your own power, but it will not work. The One who is going to judge you said it would not work. You were snake bitten the first time you ever told a lie, took something that wasn't yours, disobeyed your parent, cursed, had hatred in your heart toward another person, cheated, took the Lord's name in vain, and the list goes on and on. Jesus said in Matthew 5:28 that even your thoughts can condemn you. Accepting what Jesus did on the cross is the only way to prepare for the final judgment. I would not want to go through the end times without the seal of approval by God Himself upon me. That seal of approval is the blood of His Son Jesus—the Savior of the world.

Jesus said in Luke 18:10–14, "Two men went up to the temple to pray, one a Pharisee and the other a tax collector. The Pharisee stood and prayed thus with himself, 'God, I thank You that I am not like other men-extortioners, unjust, adulterers, or even as this tax collector. I fast twice a week; I give tithes of all that I possess. And the tax collector, standing afar off, would not so much as raise his eyes to heaven, but beat his breast, saying, 'God, be merciful to me a sinner!'" (NKJV). It's not your works of righteousness that impress God. It's your willingness to humble yourself before the God of all creation and admit your own weaknesses. God is not a respecter of persons. We all fall equally short of righteousness.

The Apostle Paul makes the way to Jesus plain and simple. He says in Romans 10:8–13, "But what does it say? The word is near you, in your mouth and in your heart (that is the word of faith which we preach): that if you confess with your mouth the Lord Jesus and believe in your heart that God has raised Him from the dead, you will be saved. For with the heart one believes unto righteousness, and with the mouth confession is made unto salvation. For the scripture says, 'Whoever believes on Him will not be put to shame.' For there is no distinction between Jew and Greek, for the same Lord over all is rich to all who call upon Him. For whoever calls on the name of the LORD shall be saved" (NKJV). What a simple message sent down from the Creator of the whole universe. Why would anyone say no to a gift of such great value. God did not sacrifice His Son because of our goodness. He gave His Son because of our weakness and because He loves us. God's word is sure, and His promises will never fail. In 2

Peter3:9–12 it says, "The Lord is not slack concerning His promise, as some count slackness, but is longsuffering toward us, not willing that any should perish but that all should come to repentance. But the day of the Lord will come as a thief in the night, in which the heavens will pass away with a great noise, and the elements will melt with fervent heat; both the earth and the works that are in it will be burned up. Therefore, since all these things will be dissolved, what manner of persons ought you to be in holy conduct and godliness, looking for and hastening the coming of the day of God, because of which the heavens will be dissolved, being on fire, and the elements will melt with fervent heat?" (NKJV). God will keep His promises and His words will not fail. Our part is only believing and receiving what He has done for us.

Don't get discouraged if you do not understand how to be saved. Just pray for understanding and seek Him through vigilant prayer. Jesus told a parable in Luke 18:1–8 saying, "Then He spoke a parable to them, that men always ought to pray and not lose heart, saying: there was in a certain city a judge who did not fear God nor regard man. Now there was a widow in that city; and she came to him, saying, 'Get justice for me from my adversary.' And he would not for a while; but afterward he said within himself, 'Though I do not fear God nor regard man, yet because this widow troubles me I will avenge her, lest by her continual coming she weary me'" (NKJV). Bombard God with prayer continuously until you get an answer. Ask, seek, knock, yell—just don't give up. Get His attention. The prize is well worth the effort.

The day of the Lord is coming whether you believe it or not. You can either prepare for it or perish when it does.

In these last days, I do not think that the plagues Revelation speaks of will be as we have known them from the Biblical account. Some people may not see it as I do, but I think one of the worst plagues ever to fall on this earth is already here. It's called drugs-(Meth, pain killers, heroin, and a host of other mind altering stimulants). Almost everyone I know has someone in their family affected by this plague in some fashion. Can you imagine being over-run with spiders all over your floors, walls, or even your body? I've heard the stories from people in drug-induced states over and over. How about dead people showing up out of nowhere and just come for a visit? I have seen their teeth literally rot right out of their sockets. I knew several that constantly picked at sores all over their bodies thinking they were covered in ticks or some kind of insects.

When I read about all the strange creatures in Revelations, I wonder how many people have seen them in their demented state. There seems no end to the stories I've heard from ex-addicts and the strange things that happened to them during their drug induced fantasies. The stories of what happened to their children during these times I will not mention here because it is too graphic and tragic to reveal.

This plague will take the most responsible people and turn them into monsters, thieves, and desperate liars. When it comes in, it will take away not only your first born, but all your children. It destroys your job, your home, takes away your loved ones, and ends whatever future you had planned for your life. It literally destroys everything in your life.

Meth is one of the worst of all. Almost anybody can set up a lab in their home and start producing or selling it. It is the affordable drug. It is a plague of gigantic proportion. Heroin seems to be making a tremendous comeback from the late sixties and early seventies. I remember hearing about this drug when I was a boy, and I thought it wasn't a drug of choice anymore, but deaths from this drug are rising at a tremendous rate especially in the northern part of the country. How could something like this be happening in our "civilized" society? This is a plague, and it will probably be here until the end of our world as we know it. There has to be something missing in the lives of people to allow them to cast away everything dear in their lives for a short burst of pleasure in a drug induced state.

The following paper is written by a young woman who I feel like touches the heart of an addict or alcoholic:

RELENTLESS THIRST

Thirst: a feeling we all posses at one time or another mentally, physically, soulfully, or spiritually, for some more strongly than others.

Some of us possess gaping wounds that the struggles and battles of life have slowly but surely left in us along our journeys. But what do we do with this thirst, how do we heal these wounds and missing pieces of ourselves? Simply trying to fill them is an empty labor with nothing at the end of it but more heartache and disappointment. Most of us are here because we have all been down this road to no avail, coming up empty every time.

Where does it come from? Are we born with this innate feeling that something is always missing? I personally believe that addicts and alcoholic have a thirst and a hunger stronger and much more intense than most, which is why we fill it with stronger substances, which ultimately creates a hunger so intense that we spend every waking second in an effort to fill ourselves with something, anything.... Only to feel those holes emptying once again, slowly but surely.

When we are in our addictions we see many mirages, more appealing and alluring than the last, all just offering and illusion of happiness and peace, and a short term distraction from our problems.

But there is a true watering hole amidst this limitless desert we call life. Jesus is sitting beside the water waiting for us to realize that only HE can offer us the water of life, filled with grace and mercy.

Many of us reach this place at the very end of ourselves, dragging ourselves, practically panting for just a drop of something to quench our dehydrated selves. And when we finally get that first taste of what He has to offer us, it is like nothing we have ever felt before. A kind of love one could never possibly explain simply with words. We can grow in His love and we soon realize that the longing that has dwelled in us for as long as we can remember is beginning to be filled and our wounds don't seem to be as raw and new as they once were. And as we stand with open arms, Jesus offers us a never-ending remedy to our thirst.

The strange paradox to this is that, even in knowing and having felt everything the Holy Spirit has to offer us, we still seem drawn to those worldly things that provide, in moments of grief, overwhelming sadness, guilt, shame, and anger: only temporary fulfillment.

Just as the ocean cannot quench someone's thirst that's caught amidst the endless, unbounding waters, nor can the world possibly quench the relentless thirst and hunger that dwells within us. Jesus is the only true source to the water of life.

—Carmen Vasquez

Just as the prophet said in Daniel 12:8, "Although I heard, I did not understand" (NKJV). So do a lot of people today. They hear, but they do not understand. By now you know I do not believe in a "rapture" before the return of Jesus, or as some refer to as His second coming. It's simply not found in the scriptures. Everyone needs to make preparations in their hearts and minds for what this world is about to become. In many ways, we are witnessing the downfall of many through deception, drugs, and a turning away from God. The world will continue its fall into self indulgence and godlessness and wax ever worse. It's going according to the way it was prophesied years ago in the Bible. There is a darkness coming that the world has yet to experience. Be ready.

He also left prophecies of great hope and encouragement for those who would listen. I want to leave you with a message from the Lord Himself for the times that we will soon face if not already. In Isaiah 60:1–2, "Arise, shine; For your light has come! And the glory of the LORD is risen upon you. For behold, the darkness shall cover the earth, And the deep darkness the people; But the LORD will arise over you, And His glory will be seen upon you" (NKJV). I don't understand all things, but one thing I do understand is God will never leave us or forsake us regardless of the circumstances. We may sometimes feel He isn't paying attention, but that is where our faith in Him is tested.

About the Author

The author is a husband of thirty-one years with three children and one grandchild. He attends church in his community and has been teaching Bible classes at a women's rehab facility since 2005.

CPSIA information can be obtained
at www.ICGtesting.com
Printed in the USA
BVHW07s2349040718
520783BV00011B/840/P

9 781641 408394